Why Water's Worth It

WHY WATER'S WORTH IT

Written by: Lori Harrison
Illustrated by: Jon Harrison
Cover art and concept by: 522 Productions

Published and distributed by the Water Environment Federation in 2019.

ISBN: 978-1-57278-354-6
Printed in the United States

Small hands, BIG heroes.

Dedicated to the next generation of water protectors.

Water Hero illustration by Penelope, age 7.

This story's about water and all that it brings.

It creates life and supports living things.

Clean water keeps us healthy, strong, and fit.

We all need reliable access to it.

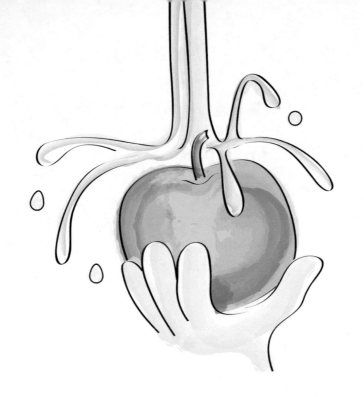

We need it to clean, to eat, and to drink.

It helps us to play, to work, and to think.

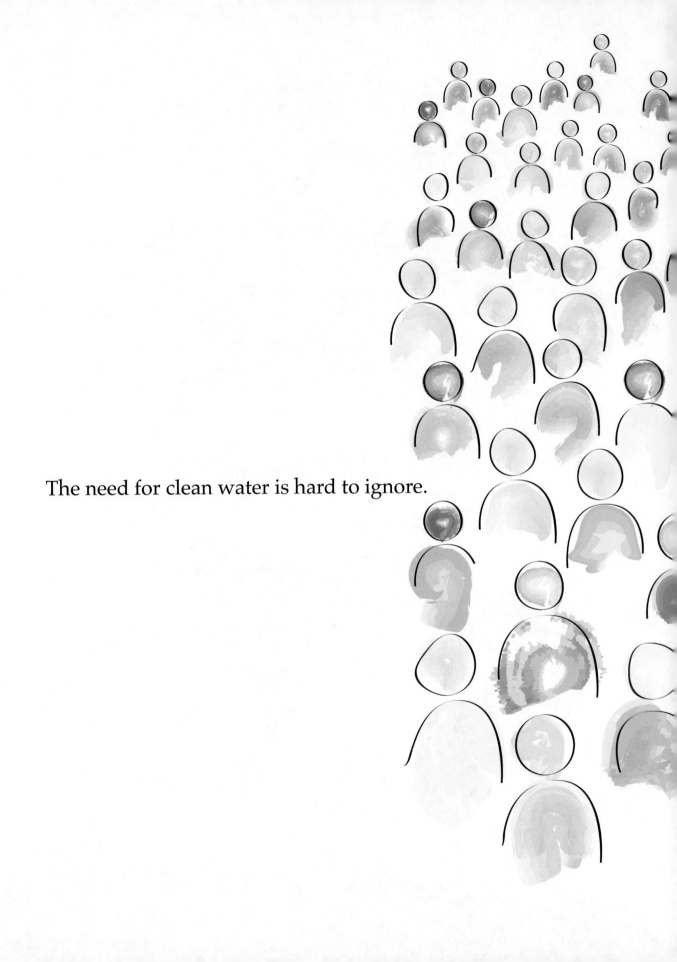

The need for clean water is hard to ignore.

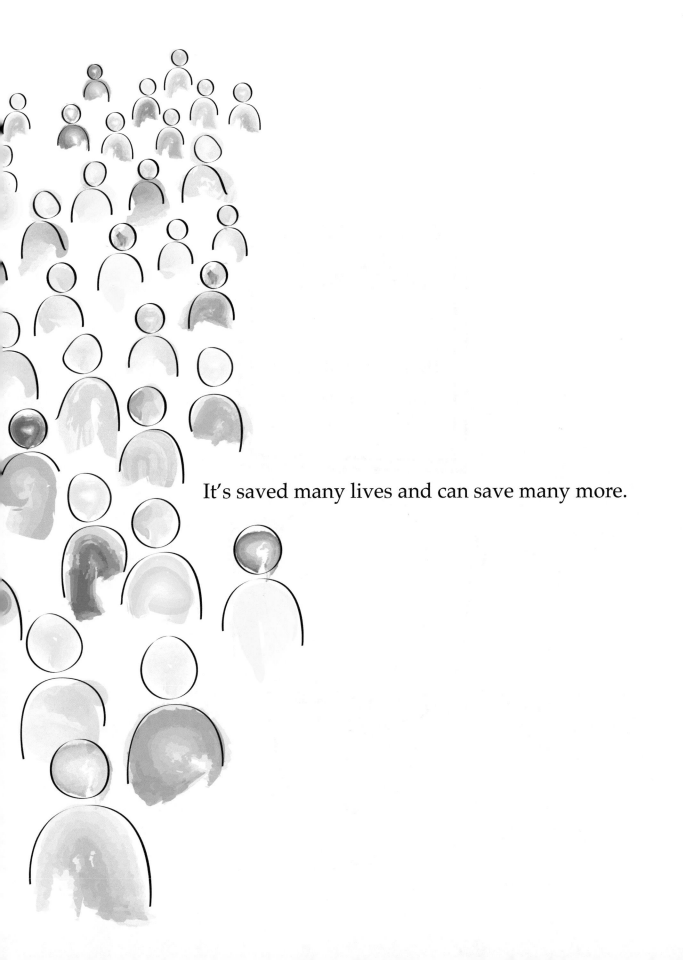

It's saved many lives and can save many more.

It needs our respect. There's a lot we can do...

to care for water and the environment too.

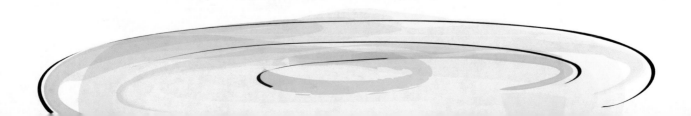

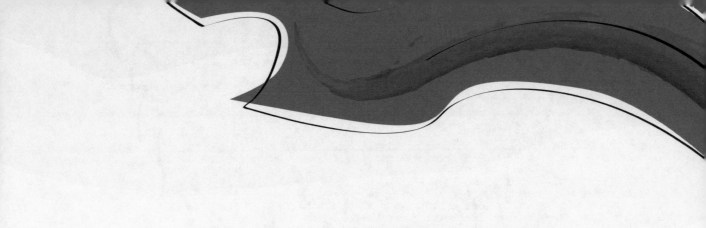

Who makes it work? What makes it go?

What does it take to make clean water flow?

It's often overlooked, unseen, and unknown.

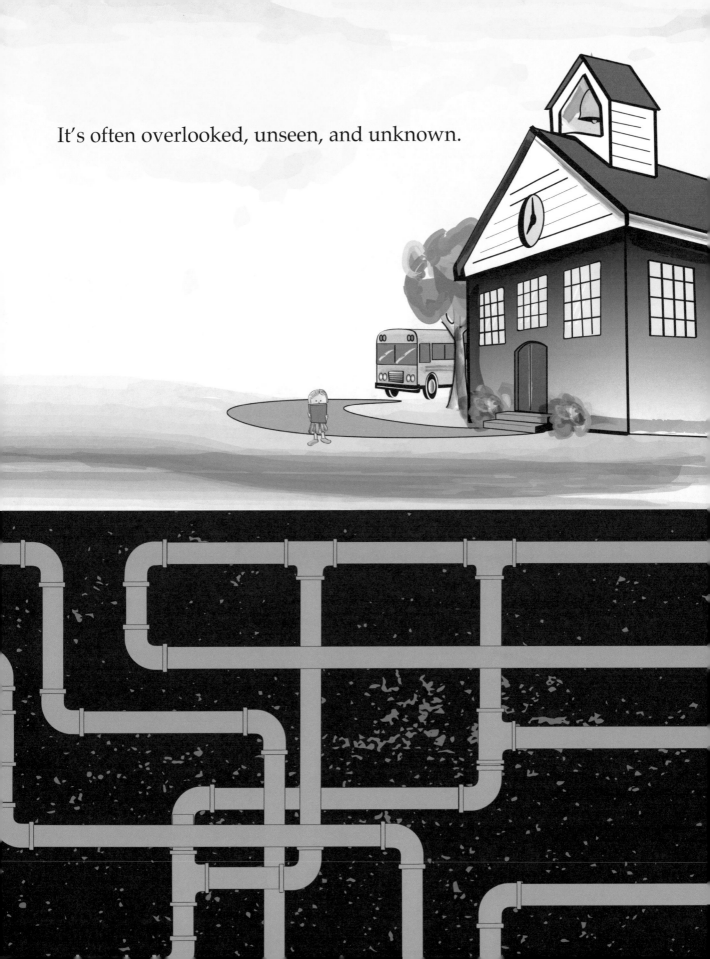

This system is vast, above and below.

It needs our investment to keep up the flow.

Passionate people who love what they do...

work hard to clean water for me and for you.

They keep it moving – with plants, pumps, and pipes...

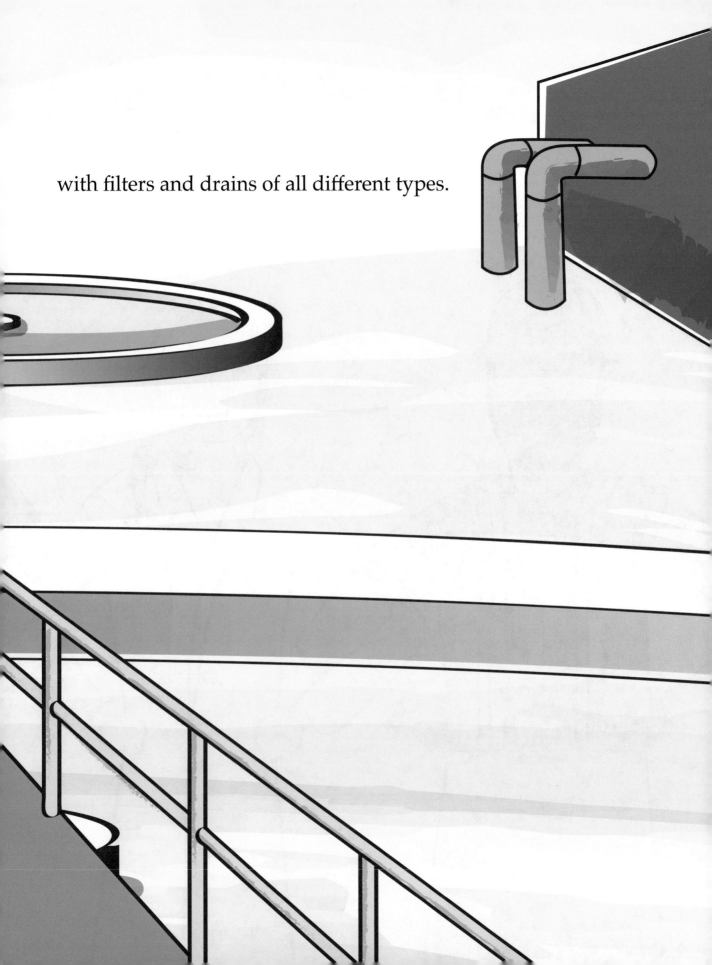

with filters and drains of all different types.

We're all in this cycle, we all live downstream.

We're in this together, we're part of this team.

We all use water...

...and create waste too.

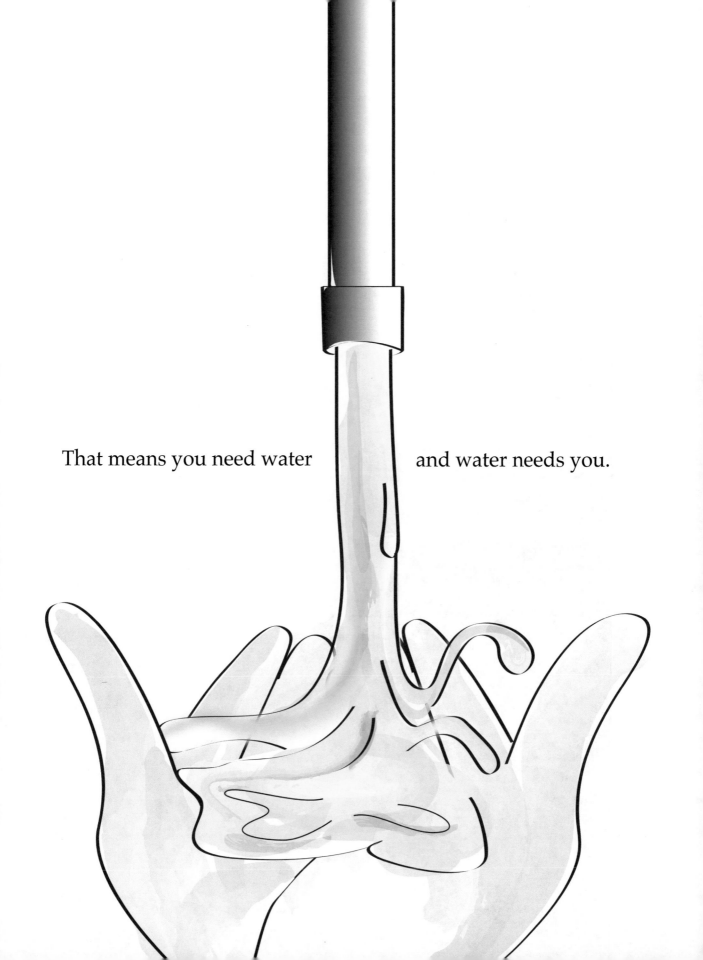

That means you need water   and water needs you.

When it's all done, at the end of the day...

a little bit of effort goes a really long way.

What about the future? What can we do...

to manage water and sustain it too?

Innovation and technology will help save the day!

We must recycle water and keep pollution away!

We make an impact with acts big and small.

We must do our part for one and for all.

All of it matters – that much is true.

That's why I hope...

Water's Worth It to you!

SMALL ACTIONS, **BIG IMPACT**
Some little tips to make a BIG difference!

Only flush the 3Ps. Everything that goes down a pipe or storm drain ends up at your local water resource recovery facility or waterbody. Limit what you flush to (toilet) paper, pee, and poo — and responsibly dispose of, or recycle, the rest.

Read through your family's water/wastewater bill with your parents and challenge everyone in your house to reduce your water footprint. Your community and our planet will thank you!

Turn off the water while brushing your teeth.

Set a timer and try to limit showers to 5 minutes. It takes 36 gallons of water to fill up the average-sized bathtub. By taking a 5-minute shower instead, you could save twice as much water!

Tweak the leak. A leaky toilet wastes about 200 gallons of water per day. Ask an adult to help you put a drop of food coloring in your toilet tank. If the color shows up in the bowl without flushing, you have a leak!

Install a rain barrel and use the water you collect to water your garden.

Scoop your pet's poop! Then put it in the trash.

Grow what you know. Look up resources online, visit the library, or ask an adult to take you on a field trip to your local facility to learn how water, wastewater, and stormwater is managed where you live.

Participate in community cleanup days, environmental festivals, or water awareness days.

Choose to reuse. Swap your single-use plastic and paper products for reusables like stainless steel water bottles and drinking straws, cloth shopping bags, silicon or beeswax storage bags, and planet-friendly bamboo toothbrushes.

Thank a Water Hero! Write a letter, make a card, or send an e-mail to the water professionals in your hometown and thank them for the important work they do every day — making sure you always have reliable access to clean, safe water and wastewater services!

YOU NEED WATER. WATER NEEDS YOU.

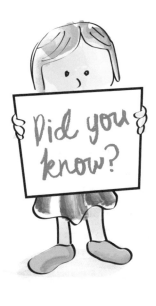

Did you know?

There is no "new" water. You drink the same water that T-rex drank over 66 million years ago.

Humans can live several weeks without food but only a few days without water. That's because our bodies are 65 to 70% water — even our bones are about 31% water!

The collection and treatment of water and wastewater is recognized as the most important way to protect public health.

The Egyptians were the first people to record methods for treating water. These records date back to 400 A.D. They cleaned water by boiling it over a fire, heating it in the sun, or by dipping a heated piece of iron into it.

Water professionals at water resource recovery facilities use innovation and technology to treat wastewater while producing valuable resources like clean water, renewable energy, natural fertilizer, nutrients, and fuel.

The first signs of water and wastewater infrastructure – the pipes and drains that keep the water flowing – can be traced back to more than 5,000 years ago. The 2,500-year-old Cloaca Maxima in Rome, Italy, is one of the oldest wastewater and stormwater systems still in use today!

The United States has more than 800,000 miles of water pipes and 700,000 miles of wastewater pipes. Together, they can circle the whole world about 60 times!

Sending anything but used water and the 3Ps down the drain can cause big problems! Fatbergs, which are massive blobs of fat, food, and wipes, have clogged and broken sewers. In London, England, one was the size of a bus…another as big as a blue whale!

Everyone must learn to recycle, reuse, and reduce waste. If we don't act now, we might end up producing 70% more trash than we do today, including filling up the oceans with more plastic (by weight) than fish!

Green infrastructure, such as permeable (sponge-like) pavement and rain gardens, helps control stormwater and eases pressure on water collection systems. It mimics the natural water cycle by capturing water, filtering out pollutants, and reducing runoff into oceans, lakes, rivers, streams, and ponds.

recycle, reuse... reduce

Sources:
The World Bank, "What a Waste 2.0: A Global Snapshot of Solid Waste Management to 2050"
www.sewerhistory.org
www.watersworthit.org/resources
www.wef.org/resources/for-the-public/value-of-water/

About the Water Environment Federation

The Water Environment Federation (WEF) is a not-for-profit technical and educational organization of 35,000 individual members and 75 affiliated Member Associations representing water quality professionals around the world. Since 1928, WEF and its members have protected public health and the environment. As a global water sector leader, our mission is to connect water professionals; enrich the expertise of water professionals; increase the awareness of the impact and value of water; and provide a platform for water sector innovation. To learn more, visit www.wef.org.

WATER'S WORTH IT.

RESPECT EFFORT PASSION HEALTH FUTURE

About WATER'S WORTH IT®

WATER'S WORTH IT is a broad-based messaging campaign from the Water Environment Federation that helps bring attention to the value and importance of clean water and the infrastructure that supports it; the essential work of water professionals; and the need for everyone who uses water to help protect it for today and the future. You Need Water. Water Needs You. To learn more and to download the accompanying Why Water's Worth It video PSA, visit www.WatersWorthIt.org.